Themes

Why pray the Psalms in time of Dementia? An introduction

My first experience of dementia was when as a child I visited my grandmother. Beloved Grandma, Isabel South, was a quiet and lovely woman born in Battersea, London, in the late 19th Century. She was the youngest of thirteen children. Late in her life, she coped with living on her own after the death of my grandfather, William. On one of our regular family visits when I was 10 years old, we arrived just as she was looking for her woolly hat. She was mortified to find she had placed it on the teapot in the cupboard and while we all laughed, even as a child I could see the worry in her eyes.

I have been a Methodist minister for many years, serving in a number of church appointments in England and Wales. Pastoral visiting has always been a priority. For a number of those years I held a variety of chaplaincy appointments, just a few hours each week, working in hospitals, prisons and in mental health care. It was in the contact with patients and staff in the world of mental health that I found a home.

My current work as a chaplain in Oxfordshire brings challenge and privilege every day. I work as part of the Older Adult Community Mental Health Team, visiting people in their homes, supporting them in difficult times. My role within the national College of Health Care Chaplains Mental Health Chaplains' Forum also brings a wider perspective.

For those struggling against dementia, lives may be changing from activity and fullness into times of struggle and confusion.

Some gradually disappear from society, their outlook shrinking to the size of their room. Many are without a formal diagnosis of dementia. And yet so much wonderful care is given. Carers offer compassion to their loved ones often at great personal cost. How can we set out to discover something calm and hopeful beyond all pain and suffering? Our humble search is for reconciliation with what is happening to us and even peace. Anxiety and depression are often present in dementia; where can one look for signs of

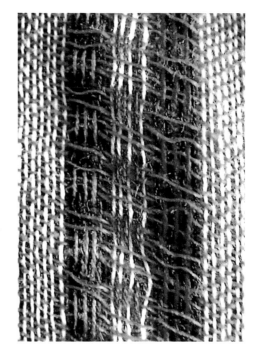

hope in a very distressing situation? I am convinced that every person has deep within them a spirituality, whether in listening to music, in artistic endeavour, in poetry, in sitting in a garden, in countless other ways too. For some this spirituality is expressed in a religious faith. This may be where the Psalms play their part as we join with the wider Church. Down through long years and in every part of the world there have been those who sing and pray the Psalms together. We can discover a profound communion with one another and with our loving God as we pray the Psalms.

As chaplains we come close to people as they struggle to make sense of their lives, as we share the experience of those caught up in dementia. Professionals, families and friends, all play their part sometimes in extreme situations. We see people needing help in a chaotic situation and we can accompany them very simply out of our own poverty until they reach calmer waters; this is a privilege that every chaplain will recognise. We know that there are countless acts of kindness and a simple humanity that make up a life, and a small gesture or word of comfort can make a great difference. A quiet

humour can transform a dire situation, with the knowledge that we all face the same dilemmas and we all need to be loved.

Personally I have found being with those encountering dementia something quite beautiful. The essence of a life comes to the fore, and a trust can be shared. Dementia itself is a most awful illness, and it comes as a terrible blow. It changes lives, disrupting a whole family, and sweeping away memories once held dear. Incredibly, something good can emerge; hope is a deep instinct and may be found in the simple pleasure of the present moment. Precious memories, so cherished, are handed over to be carried by others. Thankfully too the more distressing memories in our lives will fade and there can be a real sense of letting go of some of the things we may have struggled with for years.

Everything can be offered in trust to God, the One who never sends suffering or distress, but who always stays close by us. Our Christian faith reminds us that Jesus Christ through his Incarnation knew what it was to feel despair and fear, and he experienced death itself. His resurrection began a new chapter in our human history, new life offered to every person without exception.

This book is intended to be read by those whose lives are touched by dementia; you may have memory loss yourself, or be a carer supporting a loved one. You may work with those who have dementia. Here are words of comfort; the simple prayers can be offered alone or together. Such a moment can bring refreshment and hope as we realise that we are not alone and have not been forgotten.

Jean Fletcher

An introduction

Twenty four of the psalms have been highlighted, especially to invite us to read the whole psalm.

Why have I chosen these particular psalms? These psalms are 'famous' and for good reason. There is a depth and beauty in the words, and here are prayers which tell of our human condition. Whether we lie awake at night, or stand in wonder at creation; whether we want to complain to God, or rest simply in his forgiveness, here are words to express our deepest desires. I have described each psalm by a short heading, and we can soon see that here are words for every situation, inviting us to experience for ourselves the love of God.

A Daily Prayer

One of the lovely gifts that we can have in life is a pattern of daily prayer, and for some this comes to life when shared with a community. Many of us using this book may not have that opportunity or at least have times in our lives when prayer is not part of our daily life.

This is an invitation for us to set out again, praying a daily office that has simple words of thanksgiving. The prayers below are for the morning or the evening, but can be offered at any time.

This daily office can be read as we sit in our favourite chair, and we can prepare this space by putting an object in front of us that means a lot to us. For some this might be an icon, a religious image, or perhaps simply a leaf or stone that we have been given.

We read the words at a steady pace, so that we can let them sink deeply into us and we always begin with words of praise. God may feel far from us yet we trust in His love.

First Prayer of the Day

Psalm 100

Make a joyful noise to the Lord, all the earth.
    Worship the Lord with gladness;
    come into his presence with singing.
Know that the Lord is God.
    It is he that made us, and we are his;
    we are his people, and the sheep of his pasture.
Enter his gates with thanksgiving,
    and his courts with praise.
    Give thanks to him, bless his name.
For the Lord is good;
    his steadfast love endures forever,
    and his faithfulness to all generations.

Glory to God, Source of all Being,
Eternal Word and Holy Spirit:
As it was in the beginning is now
and shall be for ever. Amen.

The night has passed, and the day lies open before us;
let us pray with one heart and mind.

Silence for a moment.

As we rejoice in the gift of this new day,
so may the light of your presence, O God,
set our hearts on fire with love for you;
now and for ever.
Amen.

We choose one of the psalms to read.

Glory to God, Source of all Being,
Eternal Word and Holy Spirit:
As it was in the beginning is now
and shall be for ever. Amen.

We read a short reading from the Bible – a favourite passage.

A prayer:
We pray for God's blessing upon ourselves,
upon those we love, upon our world.

The Lord's Prayer:
Our Father, who art in heaven,
hallowed be thy name;
thy kingdom come;
thy will be done;
on earth as it is in heaven.
Give us this day our daily bread.
And forgive us our trespasses,
as we forgive those who trespass against us.

And lead us not into temptation;
but deliver us from evil.
For thine is the kingdom,
the power and the glory,
for ever and ever.
Amen.

An Ending to the Day

**Based upon A SONG OF OUR TRUE NATURE
by Julian of Norwich, 14th Century:**

Christ reveals our frailty and our falling
    our trespasses and our humiliations.
Christ also reveals his blessèd power,
    his blessèd wisdom and love.

He protects us tenderly and sweetly
    when we are in greatest need.
He raises us in spirit
    and turns everything to glory and joy without ending.

We are all bound to God by a beautiful grace.

And this grace is for all the world,
because it is a gift from our precious Lord Christ.
This has been given by Jesus Christ
so we may remember that we are loved. Amen.

Glory to God, Source of all Being,
Eternal Word and Holy Spirit:
As it was in the beginning is now
and shall be for ever. Amen.

A prayer:
Ever Loving God,
we remember before you
times when we have felt separated from you.
Make us whole by your Spirit
and help us to step out again with Jesus Christ our Lord. Amen.

We choose one of the psalms to read.

Glory to God, Source of all Being,
Eternal Word and Holy Spirit:
As it was in the beginning is now
and shall be for ever. Amen.

We read a short reading from the Bible, a favourite passage.

Silence for a moment.

A prayer:
We pray for God's blessing upon ourselves,
upon those we love, upon our world.

The Lord's Prayer
Our Father, who art in heaven,
hallowed be thy name;
thy kingdom come;
thy will be done;
on earth as it is in heaven.
Give us this day our daily bread.
And forgive us our trespasses,
as we forgive those who trespass against us.
And lead us not into temptation;
but deliver us from evil.
For thine is the kingdom,
the power and the glory,
for ever and ever.
Amen.

EARLY
DAYS......

What is
happening
to
me?

Psalm 3

'But you, O Lord, are a shield around me.'

When everything is thrown into disarray, when confusion grows, God is especially close to his children. His protection is as a shield, and nothing can break through to harm us.

Psalm 9

'You are the one who lifts me up from the gates of death, so that that I may recount all your praises.'

When we cannot manage by ourselves, God comes in his infinite and tender mercy, to raise us up. This happens again and again throughout our lives, and then beyond our very life, when we pass through death.

Psalm 11

'His eyes behold, his gaze examines humankind.'

Everything around us can become disturbing to us, as we struggle to make sense of the world. Journeys which once we took without a second's thought, now become impossible and our world shrinks to the size of our room. How frightening this would be, but for the loving gaze of Jesus Christ, who never forsakes us.

Psalm 28

'Hear the voice of my supplication, as I cry to you for help.'

Here is a prayer which calls out to God; to the One who knows our every fear and worry, who will come and bring us calm, inviting us to rest in his love.

Psalm 31

'I had said in my alarm, "I am driven far from your sight." But you heard my supplications when I cried out to you for help.'

Being alarmed can be a terrifying experience; we fear the worst, we cannot see the way ahead and feel ourselves to be alone. But God will always listen to our cry and he comes to us at the darkest moment to bring us his peace.

Psalm 46

'God is our refuge and strength, a very present help in trouble. Therefore we will not fear...Be still, and know that I am God!'

When we are agitated there will be movement and distraction, but as we calm the centre of our lives, the stillness becomes possible. Only then can we rest in God, receiving his blessing and discovering that we are loved.

Psalm 49

'But God will ransom my soul from the power of Sheol, for he will receive me. Selah.'

Light will always overcome the darkness, and love will always prevail over the very worst that can happen. Even when we experience the lowest depths of despair or anguish, our God will reach out to lift us up into something new, more than we could have imagined.

Psalm 51

'Have mercy on me, O God, according to your steadfast love;
according to your abundant mercy blot out my transgressions...
Create in me a clean heart, O God, and put a new and right spirit
within me.'

**Even when things have gone wrong, we can hope in God's
steadfast love. No one is perfect, and our very frailty may help us
to receive God's forgiveness, in all humility.**

Psalm 59

'For you have been a fortress for me and a refuge in the day of my
distress.'

**Where do we turn in time of distress? To whom can we turn?
When Jesus asked his disciples ' Do you also wish to go away?' we
can hear the distress in his voice. Peter replied 'Lord, to whom can
we go? You have the words of eternal life.' We are always kept safe
in the loving care of our Lord.**

Psalm 88

'O Lord, God of my salvation, when at night, I cry out in your
presence, let my prayer come before you; incline your ear to my cry.'

**The prayers of the night are precious, bringing us especially close
to our loving God. When pain and restlessness are upon us, a
simple prayer can calm us, creating within a trust, as we wait upon
God in the dark hours of the night. We give thanks that our God
always listens to our cry from the heart.**

Psalm 102

'Hear my prayer, O Lord; let my cry come to you. Do not hide your face from me in the day of my distress.'

A famous 17th Century prayer has the words 'If I forget Thee this day O Lord, do not thou forget me.' This simple prayer reminds us that God is always ready to listen, and is waiting for us when we turn to him. The struggles of the day can take our attention; Christ is silently and lovingly waiting for us to remember him.

Psalm 109

'With my mouth I will give great thanks to the Lord; I will praise him in the midst of the throng. For he stands at the right hand of the needy.'

We are often asked 'How are you? And our immediate reply is nearly always 'Fine!' But God comes into our lives in a deeper way, and stands alongside us in every situation. When we feel forlorn and lost, Jesus is there; when our strength is all gone, the Holy Spirit lifts us up; God never abandons us. We give our thanks for His goodness to us.

Psalm 116

'The Lord protects the simple; when I was brought low, he saved me. Return, O my soul, to your rest, for the Lord has dealt bountifully with you.'

Our experiences in life have a huge impact upon us, and sometimes everything seems so complicated and difficult that we do not know which way to turn. The reminder that our Lord protects the simple hearted comes as a beautiful blessing. Our Lord will save us, even from the lowest point; we can always set out again and again in His love.

Psalm 1

'They are like trees, planted by streams of water.'

Everyone needs to have connection one with another, for there to be a full life. Just as a tree is nurtured being close to the stream, so our lives are nourished in being with others. Now, in this present moment, dementia cannot hold back the stream of love flowing around and within us.

Psalm 25

'The friendship of the Lord is for those who fear him, and he makes known his covenant to them.'

We welcome our friends with great gladness of heart. We may not be able to remember past times, but in this present moment we give thanks for those who love us. Sometimes they are far from us, physically or mentally, yet we may rekindle the friendship at the moment of greatest need. Picking up from where we left off – that indeed is a gift too.

Psalm 27

'The Lord is my light and salvation: whom shall I fear? Wait for the Lord: be strong, and let your heart take courage; wait for the Lord!'

This beautiful Psalm is all about light. If we see the way, it will not be so daunting for us. If, in dementia, there are those who have confidence in us and who will stay with us, then our fears may be lessened.

Psalm 32

'Therefore let all who are faithful offer prayer to you: at time of distress, the rush of mighty waters shall not reach them.'

Water is a very powerful element, and can sweep away whole communities. In time of dementia it can seem as if everything is being swept away, all our memories and ideas that we hold dear. God know us completely and will always remain alongside us. A simple prayer quite beyond words, here and now, can unite us in a very deep way with our loving God.

Psalm 34

'I sought the Lord and he answered me, and delivered me from all my fears. Look to him and be radiant.'

This whole psalm is very beautiful in its words of trust in times of trouble. An Early Church Father, Irenaeus, said 'God calls us to joy, not to gloom.' Life can be transformed by our simple attitude of prayer and praise.

Psalm 52

'But I am like a green olive tree in the house of God. I trust in the steadfast love of God forever and ever.'

How is it possible to stand firm in times of change and disarray? We may feel as though everything will be taken away, but a tree has deep roots, and a green olive tree must be one of the most enduring and beautiful of all trees.

Psalm 62

'For God alone my soul waits in silence; from him comes my salvation. Trust in him at all times, O people; pour out your heart before him: God is a refuge for us.'

As we face an extreme sadness or a sublime happiness, we may sometimes say 'I have no words for this.' Perhaps it is then that we are closest to God, the One who never insists that we put into words those things which are beyond our reasoning; we can rest in absolute trust, in silence, in the Word.

Psalm 71

'Do not cast me off in the time of old age; do not forsake me when my strength is spent. O God from my youth you have taught me and I still proclaim your wondrous deeds.'

This psalm may touch a nerve! As we move from the summer days of a full life of activity, to the autumn mists of our remaining days, we may experience abandonment. We worry that we are a nuisance to those who care for us; and everything we once held dear seems lost. It is at this time that God remains especially close to his little children whom he loves so dearly.

Psalm 97

'The Lord loves those who hate evil; he guards the lives of his faithful.'

We receive God's love throughout our whole lives. When illness comes, when dementia strikes, we may feel very vulnerable indeed. It is then that we can allow God to 'guard the lives of his faithful' as we trust in His love.

Psalm 99

'He spoke to them in the pillar of cloud; they kept his decrees.'

In the Exodus, when God's people were being rescued from slavery, they were led through the wilderness by a pillar of cloud by day, and a pillar of fire by night. They were never in danger of being lost. The relationship with God was a covenant of love, a giving and receiving in trust, and they could travel by day or by night. We too can come close to God in the day or in the night.

Psalm 101

'I will sing of loyalty and justice; to you, O Lord, I will sing.'

Loyalty is a very beautiful attribute. It is silent and constant. One who is loyal does not speak ill of their friend, but upholds them by a simple trust. To suffer disloyalty is painful indeed; but we can look to the good and choose to speak of another in loyalty.

Psalm 105

'Seek the Lord and his strength; seek his presence continually.'

A man in his forgetfulness remarked 'The person I miss the most, is me.' In this sentence we see a whole world turned upside down. When everything, even our own identity, seems to be disappearing, we may feel completely alone. It is at just such a moment that our Lord will come, and silently, lovingly, bring His strength. His presence with us is the one secure point in our lives, and for this we are thankful, especially in times of sadness.

Psalm 125

'As the mountains surround Jerusalem, so the Lord surrounds his people, from this time on and forevermore.'

Mountains are there for a very long time and are a sign of great strength. We may feel especially tiny and fragile when we consider the mountains. If the Lord surrounds his people as with the beauty and strength of the mountains, then we know that nothing ultimately can harm us.

Psalm 139

'Where can I go from your spirit? Or where can I flee from your presence? If I ascend to heaven, you are there; if I make my bed in Sheol, you are there.'

We are reminded that God knows us through and through, across the whole range of our lifetime. This could be a terrible burden, but for the wonderful spirit of humility that marks the love of God for all people. Nothing is beyond his tender reach.

Psalm 142

'I pour out my complaint before him, I tell my trouble before him. Bring me out of prison, that I may give thanks to your name.'

Jesus spoke to Peter: 'When you were younger, you used to fasten your own belt and go wherever you wished. But when you grow old, you will stretch out your hands, and someone else will fasten a belt around you and take you where you do not wish to go.' This imprisonment can take many forms in our own lives. Jesus invited Peter at that same moment 'Follow me'. Here is an invitation from Jesus to each one of us. 'Follow me.'

Psalm 6

'Turn, O Lord, save my life; deliver me for the sake of your steadfast love.'

Even in the most difficult of circumstances, love finds a way. When our courage fails and we long for death, something new will emerge. When precious memory is impaired and all seems lost, something new can be created within us.

Psalm 10

'Why, O Lord, do you stand far off? Why do you hide yourself in times of trouble?'

When illness overtakes us we may feel alone and unloved. Dementia can make us feel isolated and even abandoned, even our memories have fled away! But as in the Psalm, we can make a discovery: 'You hear, O Lord, the desire of the afflicted, you encourage them and listen to their cry.' We are always within the embrace of our loving God.

Psalm 16

'You show me the path of life. In your presence there is fullness of joy.'

The Chinese proverb reminds us that 'every journey begins with one small step'. As we travel on the journey of life we find that we set out on the path of life time and time again. Each time we take one small step of trust, we draw closer to Jesus, discovering the joy that awaits us.

Psalm 21

'For the king trusts in the Lord, and through the steadfast love of the Most High he shall not be moved.'

Sometimes we may need to make a stand. It could be against an international injustice, or against something we know to be wrong in our own sphere of life. King David as a boy had stood firm against Goliath the giant. Now in this psalm the King is remembering the strength of the Lord and the blessings that he brings.

Psalm 38

'O Lord, all my longing is known to you; my sighing is not hidden from you...make haste to help me, O Lord of my salvation.'

This psalm speaks of repentance and the receiving of forgiveness. There may be regrets within our lives, and although nothing can change the events of the past, our attitude may yet be transformed and healed. The Lord our God will help us to do this.

Psalm 44

'If we had forgotten the name of our God, or spread out our hands to a strange god, would not God discover this? Redeem us for the sake of your steadfast love.'

Our lives are full of struggle, and perhaps fear and guilt too, but somewhere beyond the suffering, there lies a place of peace and light which we may not yet have reached. It remains before us as a sure hope.

Psalm 55

'Cast your burden on the Lord, and he will sustain you; he will never permit the righteous to be moved.'

The Psalmists have a wealth to teach us about how we should bring before God the manifold sufferings of our lives. Serious illness, the depths of abandonment, persecution and every conceivable trouble – the Psalms know them all. And it is not only our personal suffering, it is the suffering of the whole community that God will endure with us. He brings light into dark places.

Psalm 60

'Give victory with your right hand, and answer us, so that those whom you love may be rescued.'

This Psalm has a heading which describes violent times: 'when Joab on his return killed twelve thousand Edomites in the Valley of Salt' – violent times of upheaval and change. We too may face scenes of change, of emotional devastation and suffering in our personal lives. We all need to be rescued, and we can learn to place our confidence in our loving God, that in the end all that is good will prevail.

Psalm 69

'Save me, O God, for the waters have come up to my neck, I sink in deep mire where there is no foothold; Answer me, O Lord, for your steadfast love is good; according to your abundant mercy, turn to me.'

This cry comes from the heart where perhaps a guilt has lodged itself, whether from the past or in the present moment. Just as the weight of water can hinder our movement, so guilt can constrict and darken a life. Then Christ comes and lifts us up, helping us to move forward through his waters of forgiveness.

Psalm 78

'They forgot what he had done, and the miracles he had shown them. He led them to safety, so that they were not afraid.'

This Psalm in fact does not address God at all! How then are we pray it? We can make it our own when we allow that what God has done for his people, he has done for us. His care for us will always be shown to us in his Son, Jesus, even if we forget the exact detail of it all. We rest in His love.

Psalm 81

'In distress you called, and I rescued you; I would feed you with the finest wheat, and with honey from the rock I would satisfy you.'

Sometimes our feelings of distress become so habitual that we hardly want to be rescued; even when things are difficult, they are at least familiar to us. But God's promise of a deep nourishing can soften our resolve to stay in the dark, and we may allow ourselves to be rescued after all. The lovely surprise of God's loving care awaits us.

Psalm 82

'Give justice to the weak and the orphan; maintain the right of the lowly and the destitute. Rescue the weak and the needy.'

There are countless numbers of people who have need of help. Life can bring many sufferings, and without hope we could not go on. It is when we rely upon God's saving grace that we make the surprising discovery of a new life within, a blessing which can never be overcome.

Psalm 106

'O give thanks to the Lord, for he is good; for his steadfast love endures forever.'

It has been said 'All things change, God never changes'. Changes which come upon us in life can be for the good or for the ill. When things go well, we share our happiness; when things go wrong, we know that Jesus will be especially close by, helping and strengthening us for the difficult road ahead.

Psalm 118

'Out of my distress I called on the Lord: the Lord answered me and set me in a broad place. The stone that the builders rejected has become the chief cornerstone.'

A question can come into our minds, 'How can I keep going when no one cares whether I live or die?' For nearly every person someone does care; whether we are alone or with others, God will tend our wounds. Whatever deep rejection we have suffered, we can discover that we are precious in the eyes of God.

Psalm 129

'The Lord is righteous; he has cut the cords of the wicked.'

There is something very straight forward about this psalm. God will have nothing to do with the wicked, with evil, with hatred. Instead, God brings His forgiveness into our lives. When those who have suffered an evil tragedy speak only words of love, we can but wonder and learn from them. Lord, help us always to see the good in others and to rejoice in them.

Psalm 134

'Come, bless the Lord, all you servants of the Lord, who stand by night in the house of the Lord!'

The night-time is very special and can bring us close to God. When we toss and turn, and sleep flees away, we may discover something beyond the anxiety; God awaits and will bring a quietness, a peace of mind and heart to us – but only if we let him!

On a level Plateau

Psalm 7

'O Lord my God, in you I take refuge.'

If we were truly alone, then we of all people should be pitied. God is a steadying presence, looking for all that is good, kind and generous in his people. He never abandons us.

Psalm 14

'The Lord looks down from heaven on humankind to see if there are any who are wise, who seek after God.'

Our understanding of 'God up there' and of us 'down here' may have changed, as we discover God around and within. But the distance is huge between our tiny efforts, and the creative blaze of God. Without his Son, Jesus, we could hardly bridge the gap, yet in his presence we can discover an ever deepening wisdom and a loving relationship. We give our thanks.

Psalm 15

'O Lord, who may abide in your tent? Who may dwell on your holy hill?'

In this vision of welcome and hospitality, our whole life becomes a single act of worship, a sacrifice of thanksgiving. God always accepts the offering of our life of praise and brings his salvation. There is nowhere we would rather be, than safely abiding in his tent, set on holy ground.

Psalm 19

'Let the words of my mouth and the meditation of my heart be acceptable to you, O Lord, my rock and my redeemer.'

This is one of three Psalms which dwell upon the Law – the other two are Psalms 1 and 119. Here is an invitation to open our eyes to the Law as a blessing. Law is seen as the whole redemptive action of God, leading to obedience and new life. Children love to know where they are and what they can do; we are just the same, and are guided by God's Law of love.

Psalm 26

'My foot stands on level ground: in the great congregation I will bless the Lord.'

Stony ground with a slope can be very hard upon which to walk and stand. There is relief when the ground softens to a level path. Then it is possible to move forward in confidence, even when we do not fully know the destination. We can trust in God.

Psalm 37

'But the meek shall inherit the land, and delight themselves in abundant prosperity...for the Lord loves justice; he will not forsake his loved ones.'

God provides a prayer for us to offer from within our earthly needs. A prayer for daily bread encompasses the whole realm of our physical life; so also the prayer for life and health are a cry to be sustained by God's mercy and care.

Psalm 63

'My soul is satisfied as with a rich feast, and my mouth praises you with joyful lips when I think of you on my bed, and meditate on you in the watches of the night.'

Food and sleep – two essentials! We rejoice in those times of sharing a meal, a cup of tea or an ice-cream. Such simple pleasures can bring us much joy. And then we may have a nap or a deep sleep; both help us to rest and then to set out again in our life.

Psalm 72

'May he be like rain that falls on the mown grass, like showers that water the earth. For he delivers the needy when they call, the poor and those who have no helper.'

Here is a plea for justice and help for the poor; for peace, for stable government and endless glory in the king's realm. In such an uncertain world, it is good to have confidence in a loving God who will not let us go.

Psalm 75

'We give thanks to you, O God; we give thanks; your name is near. People tell of your wondrous deeds.'

Word of mouth has always been important. Whether good news or bad, we communicate with one another. Here in this psalm we have good news to share about God's love for all Creation.

On a level plateau

Psalm 85

'Steadfast love and faithfulness will meet; righteousness and peace will kiss each other.'

Working in partnership brings strength and confidence. Love and faithfulness, righteousness and peace, these are wonderful combinations of God's love, expressed towards his people. We are held in the warm embrace of God's love, but never constricted; his love brings freedom and simplicity of heart to all who look towards him.

Psalm 89

'I will sing of your steadfast love, O Lord. Forever; with my mouth I will proclaim your faithfulness to all generations.'

Our faith is not for us alone, it is to carry the Church forward towards future generations. Every baptism, every promise made, every celebration of a life, is an expression of the Truth. No darkness can overcome such a powerful love.

Psalm 104

'O Lord, how manifold are your works! In wisdom you have made them all; the earth is full of your creatures.'

This Psalm is often recited at a Harvest festival service. It is a survey of the whole range of God's works and we can wonder at the beauty and glory of creation. Imagine again a beautiful place you may have seen, where you have glimpsed the Creator's hand at work.

Psalm 108

'My heart is steadfast, O God, my heart is steadfast; I will sing and make melody.'

Sometimes we may forget just how faithful we are! A lifetime of turning towards our Lord becomes a beacon of hope, in our own lives and for others too. The philosopher Socrates is said to have claimed 'If I am asked what are two and two, what can I say but four?' And in the same way, if we are asked 'what upholds your life?' what can we say but 'God's love shown to us in His Son, Jesus.'?

Psalm 123

'Have mercy upon us, O Lord, have mercy upon us.' Traditional words of the Church plead constantly 'Kyrie Eleison',

Lord have mercy. When we offer our prayers of intercession we often add the words 'Lord have mercy': we entrust those for whom we pray to God's mercy and tenderness. We always have this mercy shown to us, even when we feel undeserving of such love. We thank our Lord for his continual, merciful goodness.

Psalm 138

On the day I called, you answered me, you increased my strength of soul.'

Physical and mental strength are prized, but how do we consider the strength of our soul? This cannot be by our own efforts, but can only be a matter of grace and mercy, We are so happy that God keeps us as 'the apple of his eye'.

On a level plateau

Psalm 146

'I will praise the Lord as long as I live; I will sing praises to my God all my life long.'

King David is attributed with 73 of the 150 Psalms. It has been said that 'the very words uttered by David were at the same time being uttered in him by the Messiah who was to come. The prayers of David were also the prayers of Christ, or rather Christ himself offered them in the person of his ancestor David.' So said the great 20th Century theologian Dietrich Bonhoeffer. What mystery we find here! We enter into a long and beautiful tradition of prayer in saying the words of a Psalm.

A
handing
OVER

Psalm 2

'Happy are all those who take refuge in him.'

We all need a place of quiet calm, where we can recover ourselves and where we feel safe. Our God of love cannot be overcome by darkness or fear, and there is safety and rest in his presence. In the very act of trusting God, blessing is received.

Psalm 8

'O Lord, our Sovereign, how majestic is your name in all the earth!'

In the great scheme of creation, we are but tiny beings, but even so we can see the universe, the stars and planets; we consider the sea in its greatness and in its depths. The world is a beautiful and abundant place. So many colours to enjoy! Such beauty is poured out to bring us a glimpse of God's Creation. Our memories are safe in God's care.

Psalm 12

'The promises of the Lord are promises that are pure, silver refined in a furnace on the ground, purified seven times.'

Every event in our lives makes an impression upon us, but to remember everything would be a terrible ordeal. Our memories are selective and we keep the best of them. When dementia comes, we can hand those memories over without being anxious, because we are held by God, purified in the fire of His love.

Psalm 35

'You have seen, O Lord; do not be silent! O Lord, do not be far from me!'

How terrible it would be, if no one understood us. We may face loneliness and even betrayal, but we are never beyond the reach of God's tender mercy – 'he knows our frame, he remembers that we are dust.' All is within his care.

Psalm 39

'And now Lord, what do I wait for? My hope is in you.'

In a place of care for those with dementia, a refrain was recently heard: 'How long have I got to go on like this?' and it sounded as a psalmist's words, right from the heart. We can comfort one another by our words and gestures, and even in the darkest times it is possible to kindle a renewed hope.

Psalm 41

'My enemies wonder in malice when I will die, and my name perish. And when they come to see me they utter empty words.. but you have upheld me because of my integrity, and set me in your presence forever.'

We may try not to have any enemies, but there will always be those who disagree with us and disregard our outlook. The Lord can come and bring his comfort and joy, so that after every set-back we can set out again in trust.

Psalm 54

'Save me, O God, by your name, and vindicate me by your might. Hear my prayer, O God; give ear to the words of my mouth.'

We cannot make everything right by our own effort, it is too much for us. Thankfully our Lord Jesus has come to us, bringing his salvation, lovingly offered through his life given on the cross. His life, death and resurrection ensure our redemption; how astonishing!

Psalm 57

'I cry to God Most High, to God who fulfils his purpose for me.'

Without a purpose in life we can sink into the mire. We may wonder why we get up in the morning, and how to get through a day without purpose. Our activity may be restricted, we may not be able to remember those things we hold dear; but God always has a purpose for us. Jesus reminds us 'Love one another, as I have loved you'.

Psalm 64

'Hear my voice, O God, in my complaint; preserve my life from the dread enemy.'

A relationship that is rooted in love will allow praise and complaint to be expressed in equal measure, for nothing will hinder the flow of love. We know that life is not easy. We can tell God everything, even those things we can hardly dare tell ourselves.

Psalm 76

'Glorious are you, more majestic than the everlasting mountains.'

It is hard to imagine anything lasting longer than the mountains, they seem so solid and immovable. Yet God in his Wisdom has chosen to reveal his majestic power, and we can but wonder at this miracle of love.

Psalm 79

'How long, O Lord? Will you be angry forever? Deliver us, and forgive our sins.'

This prayer is full of repentance, a turning from all that would overwhelm us, towards the good. Our fear may be that God is angry with us, but when we look to his Son Jesus, we see only compassion and forgiveness. God has every right to be angry with those who show no mercy, but even then he offers a way that leads to the light.

Psalm 90

'So teach us to count our days that we may gain a wise heart.'

Time is a variable commodity, sometimes short, sometimes long. The days pass and we may hear it said 'every year is shorter than the last'. Nothing can stop the march of time, but we can savour the moment. Entrusting God with the past and trusting to the future, we discover that everything is within God's loving embrace.

Psalm 94

'When the cares of my heart are many, your consolations cheer my soul.'

'Pack up your troubles in your old kit bag, and smile, smile, smile!' If only it were as easy as that. We may be weighed down with so much that troubles us and we may not know which way to turn. Yet if we look towards the Lord, we receive blessings and peace, more than we could have imagined possible.

Psalm 122

'Peace be within your walls, and security within your towers. For the sake of my relatives and friends I will say,"Peace be within you."'

Words of blessing are something very special. If a blessing is withheld, it can lead to the distress of breaking a relationship. But a blessing freely given speaks of generosity of spirit, of rejoicing in another's life, of peace of mind and heart. Every day, may we bless those whom we love.

Psalm 127

'Unless the Lord builds the house, those who build it labour in vain.'

This is a salutary thought – what if we have been mistaken in our lives, all these years? A saint has written, 'are there briars and thorns, the mistakes of our lives? These are added to the fire that refines, leading us to discover the truth of being loved.' Here is a real comfort, nothing is 'lost' but all goes to feed the fire of love.

A handing over

Psalm 128

'May you see your children's children. Peace be upon Israel!'

Here is a prayer asking that the generations may flourish, that we should see our children, our grandchildren and even our great-grandchildren as they grow and develop. A little child can bring such joy! They love us and accept us just as we are. Then as we grow old we can hand responsibility over to those who are young and full of energy, rejoicing in their strength and confidence. It is not easy for them, and we pray for those who care about us

Psalm 141

'Let my prayer be counted as incense before you, and the lifting of my hands as an evening sacrifice.'

St. Paul wrote to the church in Corinth that our lives become a beautiful fragrance through knowing Jesus Christ; enhancing those around us. (2 Corinthians chapter 2v14) It is not for us to know how much we uphold others by our attitudes and faith, we seek only to trust in God. In the evening of our days this means that we can pray very openly, and with a simple heart, offering everything to God's merciful care.

Psalm 143

'I remember the days of old, I think about all your deeds, I meditate upon the works of your hands.'

Memories remind us of people and places we once knew. As memory fades, it may be difficult to recall that which we have cherished. God knows how much we want to remember our loved ones! He will hold our memories that are very dear to us, nothing will be lost.

DESOLATION

and LOSS

Psalm 5

'Give ear to my words, O Lord; give heed to my sighing.'

It is not easy to let go of past activity, to relinquish all that once filled our lives. Each day is a gift of new life, each moment a blessing from God. He understands us when we sigh, and brings comfort to us.

Psalm 13

'How long, O Lord? Will you forget me forever?... But I have trusted in your steadfast love; my heart shall rejoice in your salvation.'

How often we begin on a note of complaint! Life is never perfect, and we may feel overlooked. This psalm reminds us that we can always turn again towards our loving God, even when we are feeling angry or low. He will never forsake us or grow tired of us.

Psalm 18

'The cords of death encompassed me..the snares of death confronted me.'..... It is you who lights my lamp; the Lord, my God, lights up my darkness.'

To sit in the darkness can be very lonely. A lamp will brighten everything and help us to feel a fresh hope. Life will still hold many complications and we may feel ensnared by our situation, but Jesus, Light of the World, brings to us his gentleness and peace.

Psalm 22

'My God, my God, why have you forsaken me? Why are you so far from helping me, from the words of my groaning?'

Jesus prayed these words from the Cross, making them his own. Such a prayer is from his time of suffering, and may be our experience too. It was a cry from the heart and we also may cry out in despair. It would be unbearable, but for the comfort and strength given by God, who has been to such a place of suffering himself. Christ's cry upon the Cross tells us there can be no suffering on earth in which Christ is not with us, suffering and praying alongside us.

Psalm 42

'As a deer longs for flowing streams, so my soul longs for you, O God.'

Within this Psalm lies the image 'tears have been my food day and night'. How long may seem the night watch! How exhausting we find the tears of sorrow for what might have been, and what should have been in our lives. There is no going back. Our longing for peace carries us forward towards God, he who awaits us with love in his very being.

Psalm 43

'Why are you cast down, O my soul, and why are you disquieted within me? Hope in God: for I shall again praise him, my help and my God.'

There may be times when we cannot see the way ahead, when everything is in darkness. It seems that no one can help. There are no easy answers and our very soul may be in despair. The psalmist never leaves us there, but always brings a word of hope, even in dire times. For that we are thankful to God.

Psalm 113

'He raises the poor from the dust, and lifts the needy from the ash heap, to make them sit with princes, the princes of his people.'

These words are echoed in the Magnificat, (St. Luke's Gospel chapter 1) which includes the words 'He has brought down the powerful from their thrones, and lifted up the lowly.. he has filled the hungry with good things'. There is this movement, brought about by our loving God, to raise up those who are downcast and abandoned. May we allow ourselves to be lifted up out of despair; may we discover that we are worthy of love and respect, just as shown to us by our Lord Jesus.

Psalm 114

'Tremble, O earth, at the presence of the Lord, who turns the rock into a pool of water, the flint into a spring of water.'

A woman remarked 'When I go to sleep at night I hope that I won't wake up, but I always do.' Here are words of despair, wanting life to end. Everything may become a struggle and we can become exhausted in our very spirit. In the desert Moses struck the rock and water gushed out. When we are dry and tired, God will come to us and help us to set out again. He will bring to us the water of life, even in the desert.

Psalm 120

'In my distress I cry to the Lord, that he may answer me.'

The human spirit is something quite incredible. A man facing many difficulties in his life, managed to say, 'However bad you feel, you've got to try.' His hope, his outlook was very humbling to behold. Lord, help us to try.

Psalm 124

'We have escaped like a bird from the snare of the fowlers; the snare is broken, and we have escaped.'

The history of God's people was marked by the Exodus, the journey into freedom. We may long to escape from our own limitations, from our circumstances. Just as it would seem impossible for a bird to escape from the snare, so we, amazingly, can escape from that which ensnares us; we can live a life of freedom and praise; this is something which we can choose for ourselves and God will help us.

Psalm 126

'May those who sow in tears reap with shouts of joy. Those who go out weeping, bearing the seed for sowing, shall come home with shouts of joy, carrying their sheaves.'

Whatever life brings to us, it will slip away in the blink of an eye. Our long-suffering will not be forever; only God's love is forever. There is nothing to fear, joy will be ours at the last. Lord, help us to trust in your love.

Psalm 130

'Out of the depths I cry to you, O Lord. Lord hear my voice! For with the Lord there is steadfast love, and with him is great power to redeem.'

This prayer may be offered to God from the depths of despair, but it can also be from the depths of joy. The whole of our life is gathered into God's Kingdom. It is here that a new hope can begin, even in darkest days.

Psalm 132

'O Lord, remember in David's favour all the hardships he endured.'

King David had a very difficult life, he was far from perfect, and yet he received great blessing from God. We too may bear great hardships, we too are by no means perfect. Yet, how can we respond to the blessings which God provides – do we even notice that they are there? Lord help us to receive your love.

Psalm 135

'Praise the Lord, for the Lord is good; sing to his name, for he is gracious.'

We may be reminded that 'David did not pray out of the super abundance of his own heart but from the indwelling presence of Jesus Christ.' These words come from the German theologian Dietrich Bonhoeffer. We do not have to worry about the words we bring, but we can allow a prayer beyond words to flow through the loving presence of God. He will never forsake us, even in the darkest and most frightening of times.

Psalm 136

'It is he who remembered us in our low estate, for his steadfast love endures forever.'

A man once said 'If there was a snake there on the ground, I would be lower than that snake.' Such darkness and despair could only be reached by the gentle, confident love of the one who loves us, our Lord God.

Psalm 137

'By the rivers of Babylon – there we sat down and there we wept when we remembered Zion.'

Not all our memories are of happy times. When there has been loss, separation and exile, a deep sadness can pervade our soul. Dementia may seem as though we are being sent into exile from all that is beloved and familiar. In our desolation we may not see the living stream running nearby, we may not hear the note of hope sung by those close to us. Nothing is ever rejected by God; not even our darkest times. There will never be a return to how things were before, but a stillness within us becomes a possibility.

Rediscovering JOY

Psalm 24

'Lift up your heads, O gates! And be lifted up, O ancient doors! That the King of Glory may come in.'

The Psalms were originally sung in times of procession to the Temple and there is a great sense of movement here. We may be reminded of the words sung in Steiner's 'Crucifixion' – 'fling wide the gates! fling wide the gates!....Even in an extreme moment of danger, Jesus entered Jerusalem on his way to the cross and the very gates themselves allowed the King to enter.

Psalm 30

'You have turned my mourning into dancing; you have taken off my sackcloth and clothed me with joy.'

There are so many different experiences in life, some are happy, others utterly devastating. A full life will have so many riches of memory, more than we can count. Our loving God promises that beyond all sadness, something joyful awaits.

Psalm 33

'Rejoice in the Lord, O you righteous. Sing to him a new song; play skilfully on the strings with loud shouts.'

Not all of us may consider ourselves to be righteous! Yet by the mercy and forgiveness that God brings to us through his Son, Jesus Christ, we too can sing a new song and shout our praise. No one is left out.

Psalm 45

'A wedding song: my heart overflows with a goodly theme, I address my verses to the king; my tongue is like a pen of a ready scribe.'

We see a picture of God's beauty, his wealth and power, with a bride given to him in marriage. She adorns herself and enters his house with joy. We are reminded of Jesus the wedding-day groom and the Church which belongs to him. Our memories of a marriage-day, whether our own or at the celebration for a friend, can remind us of this joy.

Psalm 47

'Clap your hands, all you peoples; shout to God with loud songs of joy.'

C.S. Lewis writes 'the most valuable thing the Psalms do for us is to express the same delight in God which made David dance.' Sometimes our prayers and praises can sound anything but joyful! Yet in the midst of many difficulties in life, King David offered his exuberant praises. Perhaps we may dare to be more open in our praise too.

Psalm 67

'May God be gracious to us and bless us and make his face to shine upon us; may God continue to bless us.'

This traditional blessing is full of a quiet confidence. We may remember times when we have given a loved one a gift, and they have been gracious in their response. This brings its own joy, in knowing ourselves to be accepted and loved. Perhaps we may think of the most beautiful gift we have ever given, or received, and we rejoice in the memory.

Psalm 73

'But for me it is good to be near God; I have made the Lord God my refuge, to tell of all your works.'

Sometimes, just to be near to one we love, is enough for us. There is no need of conversation, or explanation; we can simply be comfortable in one another's presence. So too with our loving God; we can be so glad that God's love, show to us in Jesus, is enough for us.

Psalm 80

'Restore us, O God; let your face shine, that we may be saved.'

When Moses came down from the mountain having encountered God, his face shone. That inner joy sustained him through many difficult times in the wilderness. If we will but allow it, our encounter with Jesus can transform our lives and an inner joy can help us to face those things that seem to be impossible to bear.

Psalm 93

'He has established the world; it shall never be moved.'

For those without faith, the creation of the world is seen as a random act of the universe that has come into being of its own accord. Scientists strive to explain the phenomenon of nature. Yet the beauty, the luminescence, the intricacy and the very song of the universe points towards a purpose, a creative spirit at work; we can but wonder at it all.

Psalm 95

'O come, let us sing to the Lord; let us make a joyful noise to the rock of our salvation!'

Here is a psalm of trust, celebrating God's presence with us. Other verses in this psalm remind us that God is to be found in the depths of the earth, and on the heights of the mountains; in the sea and on dry land; He is in all places and is worthy of our praise and adoration.

Psalm 98

'O sing to the Lord a new song, for he has done marvellous things.'

We can rejoice in one another when we see good lives lived out in simple joy. Such a life carries great risk, for there are those who would bring down and destroy. This was Jesus' experience too. His resurrection which followed his passion and death, have brought to us a whole new world of hope. May we enter into this new life which cannot be overcome by dementia, or even by death.

Psalm 107

'For he satisfies the thirsty, and the hungry he fills with good things.'

We may not often experience hunger and thirst and in fact the next cup of tea is never far away! But our hunger for justice and our thirst for love are much deeper. We pray for justice and peace as we think of the world around us, and we can give thanks for everyone who helps to nourish and sustain us.

Psalm 110

'The Lord is at your right hand.'

This Psalm proclaims the victory of Christ over his enemies, followed by the establishment of his kingdom and the worship of God by his people. The great Reformer, Martin Luther described this Psalm as 'the foremost among the chief psalms of our dear Lord Jesus Christ.' How extraordinary; may we read it with a new understanding.

Psalm 119

'Happy are those whose way is blameless, who walk in the law of the Lord.'

The longest Psalm! Our delight is in a whole way of life that seeks to follow the laws of God, from our beginning to our end. And from Jesus, the ultimate 'law' – "love one another as I have loved you." The repetition of the words in the Psalm are in fact variations on a theme, the love of God's Word. Just as this love can have no end, neither can the words that acknowledge it. They last our whole life long.

Psalm 145

'The Lord is gracious and merciful, slow to anger and abounding in steadfast love. The Lord is good to all, and his compassion is over all that he has made.'

This lovely psalm has been offered for long years by Jews and Christians alike. It has been said that they who take this psalm to themselves are already 'a child of the world to come' Time and again in the psalms there is this experience of God's love, here and now in the present moment, in the Kingdom of God.

Psalm 148

'Praise him, all his angels; praise him, all his host! Praise him, sun and moon; praise him, all you shining stars!'

All of creation is heard to praise our loving God. The very movement of planets and stars in the universe is said to have a harmonious sound. It would be a tragedy to miss out, to turn away. Let us be there with countless others, praising and singing together.

Psalm 150

'Praise him for his mighty deeds; praise him according to his surpassing greatness! Let everything that breathes praise the Lord!'

One hundred and fifty Psalms and every single one tells of God's love! Whether from the depths of despair or the heights of joy, we can begin again and again and always offer our prayers of hope. Our loving Lord God will always pour out his blessing upon us.

Psalm 4

'I will both lie down and sleep in peace; for you alone, O Lord, make me lie down in safety.'

The nights may be long and wakeful, rest seems to flee into the distance. In the long watch of the night, God will come with his peace and the dawn of a new day promises a fresh hope.

Psalm 17

'Guard me as the apple of the eye; hide me in the shadow of your wings.'

How wonderful to be loved and appreciated, to care for one another. This verse can be written as 'guard me as you would guard your own eyes' – reminding us that we are each something very precious, and irreplaceable.

Psalm 36

'For with you is the fountain of life; in your light we see light.'

Moses in the wilderness saw water gushing from the rock, a most unexpected miracle. Nothing could contain the generous gift of God to his people at their time of need. We too receive the same fountain of living water, now revealed in Christ himself, here within our hearts.

Psalm 48

'Great is the Lord and greatly to be praised in the city of our God. His holy mountain, beautiful in elevation is the joy of all the earth.'

This is a celebration of Jerusalem, the city of God, the great fortress of the people of God; we can see the Temple and imagine its ceremonies. God remains in the midst of his people, and now he remains in the midst of our lives too, never abandoning us and always encouraging our tiny buds of faith.

Psalm 53

'God looks down from heaven on humankind to see if there are any who are wise, who seek after God.'

Humanity must have been a disappointment to God, from Old Testament times, through the New Testament times of Jesus, right to the present day. Incredibly, God never gives up on us, but waits patiently for the day when we turn to him. His loving gaze awaits us.

Psalm 56

'This I know, that God is for me. In God, whose word I praise, in the Lord, whose word I praise, in God I trust; I am not afraid.'

St Paul wrote inspired words 'If God is for us, who is against us? He who did not withhold his own Son, but gave him up for all of us, will he not with him also give us everything else?' (Romans ch 8 v31-32). It is a brilliant thought: 'This I know, that God is for me.'

Psalm 61

'Let me abide in your tent forever, find refuge under the shelter of your wings.'

The prophet Isaiah had a vision of a tent standing with guy ropes let out and pegs strongly secured, inviting an openness of outlook from a very secure base. We may be helped in our lives if we can 'let out the guy ropes' of our opinions, whilst at the same time securing the pegs of faith in deep and fertile ground.

Psalm 68

'Father of orphans and protector of widows is God in his holy habitation. God gives the desolate a home to live in.'

Life can be very precarious, taking unexpected turns. God remains close by and brings comfort to us. The 12th Century Persian poet, Rumi, wrote 'Somewhere beyond the right and the wrong there is a garden. I will meet you there.' These are such deep words of hope.

Psalm 70

'Let all who seek you rejoice and be glad in you. You are my help and my deliverer; O Lord, do not delay!'

We do not like to be kept waiting, and impatience can spoil the day. The slower pace of old age may cause much frustration, but it may perhaps be possible to learn to embrace the moment and to receive that slow time as an invitation to reflect and give thanks.

Psalm 83

'O God, do not keep silence; do not hold your peace or be still, O God!'

We so often need to receive reassurance! In the silence we may discover a deep truth, that the stillness is a gift, not a withholding. Without times of quietness we would be distressed indeed.

Psalm 86

'But you, O Lord, are a God merciful and gracious, slow to anger, abounding in steadfast love, and faithfulness.'

Here indeed is a happy thought! Perhaps as we grow nearer to our Lord, we can display some similar characteristics, in our own lives.

Psalm 87

'Singers and dancers alike may say, "All my springs are in you."'

A song or a dance can renew the spirit, expressing that which is beyond all words. A lovely song, a lyrical dance, these are like a fresh spring of water, welling up to bring renewed hope. Perhaps we can remember a time when we danced and the world was young.

Psalm 92

'The righteous flourish like the palm tree, and grow like a cedar in Lebanon. In old age they still produce fruit; they are always green and full of sap.'

Here are words of hope. As we enter our later years, wisdom may grow, and with it new opportunities arise. Where once there was full activity, now a prayer can be offered in repose. Nothing is lost, but everything is gathered up within a long life.

Psalm 96

'O sing to the Lord a new song; sing to the Lord, all the earth.'

Here are words of celebration, repeated many times – sing! sing! sing! God comes to us, however lowly we may be, and lifts us up. It is through God's great love for His people that such a joy is possible. How terrible it would be if we were left in the depth of despair, without hope. Yet our God comes in gentleness and humility, shown to us in His son Jesus Christ, to help us at just such a time.

Psalm 112

'For the righteous will never be moved; their hearts are steady, they will not be afraid.'

There is something incredibly comforting in this psalm. It is such a wonderful idea that our hearts can be steady and that we shall not be afraid. To live in such a way is a statement of faith, helpful to us and to those around us.

Psalm 115

'The Lord has been mindful of us; he will bless us.'

Being mindful is something very modern, and at the same time very ancient. We are reminded that the past, our memories, are held safely in God's care, and that the future is His also. We have this present moment as a gift beyond compare, something very precious. We may not feel well, we may have an inner distress, but it is exactly at this time that we can invite our Lord to come and look after us

Psalm 117

'Praise the Lord, all you nations! Extol him, all you peoples! For great is his steadfast love toward us, and the faithfulness of the Lord endures forever. Praise the Lord!'

Here it is, the shortest Psalm, in its entirety. Here is the most wonderful trust in God.

Psalm 131

'But I have calmed and quieted my soul, like a weaned child with its mother, my soul is like the weaned child that is with me.'

This most beautiful psalm is full of peace and rest. At heart we are all tiny children in need of a parent's unconditional love, and we realise anew that God can fulfil that longing. Then we can truly say 'There is nowhere I would rather be', and this is a wonderful gift to us.

Psalm 140

'I know that the Lord maintains the cause of the needy, and executes justice for the poor.'

Here is a statement of great faith. Whilst we may suffer injustice and discord, the psalmist knows that the Lord remains faithful and true, so that beyond the sufferings of this life, something new will emerge. And more than that, he will stay close-by through every event in our life, so there is nothing to fear.

Psalm 20

'May He grant you your heart's desire, and fulfil all your plans.'

That which we hope for, may not come to pass. The many losses in life can wound us deeply. A beautiful prayer asks that we may have serenity in those things which cannot be changed. Perhaps our desires can change in time, and in the present moment we may simply want to be in God's loving presence. This in itself is a fulfilment.

Psalm 23

'You prepare a table before me in the presence of my enemies; you anoint my head with oil; my cup overflows.'

We strive not to have any enemies in life. But incapacity through long years, and the devastation of dementia, means that these may indeed be experienced as 'enemies'. This is a psalm about being anointed in the presence of our enemies, here a table is laid out before us, assuring us that God graciously comes to us. We can say with quiet confidence 'You are with me, your rod and your staff – they comfort me.'

Psalm 29

'The voice of the Lord is powerful; the voice of the Lord is full of majesty.'

A voice in the fullness of life is a wonderful thing. In old age we may lose that strength and certainty in our speaking. Perhaps after long years of chatter and speech, it is time to rest and ponder in our hearts those countless words we have said over the years.

Psalm 40

'I waited patiently for the Lord: he inclined to me and heard my cry.'

The theologian Dietrich Bonhoeffer had an insight – 'praying does not simply mean pouring out one's heart, it means rather – whether the heart be full or empty – finding one's way to God and talking to him. And no one can do this by himself, he needs Jesus Christ.' God remains near to us and hears our prayer, he blesses us through his Son, Jesus.

Psalm 50

'I know all the birds of the air, and all that moves in the field is mine.'

Here is a Psalm which speaks of God's mercy, of how we belong to God, and in return we express our thankfulness and trust in him. By this very prayer we receive the promise of salvation itself.

Psalm 58

'People will say, "Surely there is a reward for the righteous; surely there is a God who judges on earth."'

We like things to be fair and we are angry when the unrighteous prevail. But our complaint is known to God even before it is uttered, and all in good time his justice will win the day. We can rest in his love.

Psalm 65

'Praise is due to you, O God, in Zion; and to you shall vows be performed, O you who answer prayer!'

After a complaint, may come a moment of peace, even of praise. God knows the deepest intentions within us, and even when we fall, God will bless us and help us to rise again to a new day.

Psalm 66

'We went through fire and through water; yet you have brought us out to a spacious place.. all the earth worships you: they sing praises to you, sing praises to your name. Selah.'

The word 'selah' frequently occurs in the middle of a Psalm and probably indicates an interval. "The selah is telling us to pause and reflect diligently on the words of the Psalm, for they require a calm and tranquil soul who is able to grasp with understanding what the Holy Ghost is presenting to his thought." So wrote the great church reformer, Martin Luther. How carefully everything is prepared, to help us to rest within our loving God.

Psalm 74

'Yours is the day, yours also is the night; you established the moon and the sun.'

It's a comfort to us to know that whether it is light or dark, the Lord is there. More than that, our Creator God has brought the very universe into being. And then cares for us, each one, which is quite incredible.

Psalm 77

'I consider the days of old, and remember the years of long ago. I commune with my heart in the night; I meditate and search my spirit.'

This is a most lovely psalm for those who live with dementia. We may struggle to remember past times, and the realisation of our loss can bring tears. In the long hours of a sleepless night we may offer all our memories once held, and share a deep communion with our loving Lord.

Psalm 84

'How lovely is your dwelling place O Lord of hosts! Happy are those who live in your house, ever singing your praise. For a day in your courts is better than a thousand elsewhere.'

We may think of places where we love to be, where we can truly be at home. In fullness of life there may be many such places; in the bloom of youth we create countless places of belonging. We may walk within a special vista of mountain scenery, or catch a glimpse of the sea, we may recall a friend with whom we once spoke, or dream of the look of love we have received; all these are so precious. As we become older the memories of these times may sustain us; but then all things change and even those memories begin to fade. There is nothing to fear; everything is safe; God holds our memories for us. Nowhere is better to be than quietly to sit in God's presence, welcomed into his courts of praise.

Psalm 91

'For he will command his angels concerning you to guard you in all your ways. On their hands they will bear you up, so that you will not dash your foot against a stone.'

Many people have experienced an angel's presence, guarding and watching over them. Accident and illness may befall us, but nothing is beyond the tender care of our God, the One who cares for us.

Psalm 100

'It is he that made us, and we are his; we are his people, and the sheep of his pasture.'

This wonderful psalm speaks to us about belonging. No one is beyond the reach of God's love, no one can stray into the darkness and be lost. By singing a simple song of praise we place ourselves within the safety of God's love. Jesus said 'My sheep hear my voice and I know them, and no one shall snatch them out of my hand.' What comfort these words can bring to us.

Psalm 103

'Bless the Lord, o my soul, and do not forget all his benefits.'

Here is a picture of God's abundant provision of his gifts. This Psalm is often read at a funeral service, when a whole life is offered back to God. Here is a preparation towards eternal life, completely secure in God's love for us.

Psalm 111

'O praise the Lord! I will give thanks to the Lord with my whole heart.'

It is good to be wholehearted! Sometimes we may withhold our attention, or our affection, in order to make a point. Christ never turns the knife of conscience in our wounds, but will tenderly come to us and bring us his whole being.

Psalm 121

'I lift up my eyes to the hills - from where will my help come?' 'The Lord will keep you from all evil; he will keep your life.'

This beautiful psalm has about it a wonderful vision, full of air and light, and in that spacious place God comes to help us. We are promised that his attention rests upon us in a most loving way, that we will never be discarded or forgotten. 'He will keep your going out and your coming in.' – what constancy! what love!

Psalm 133

'How very good and pleasant it is when kindred live together in unity!'

This short psalm speaks of precious oil on the head, 'running down over the collar of his robes'. The cold winds of the European climate can hardly allow us to appreciate the refreshment and happiness of that oil, which comes as a precious gift, tendered in a hot climate. God is present in all cultures, bringing love and unity.

Psalm 144

'My rock and my fortress, my stronghold and my deliverer.'

We constantly rest in God's love, allowing Him to strengthen and save us. We know that we are not perfect, yet God remains faithful to us, right to the end of our life. And then beyond that, something awaits that is full of life and joy.

Psalm 147

'He heals the broken hearted, and binds up their wounds.'

The tenderness of God is a wonderful gift; he never wounds us as he lifts us up, but by gentle touch breathes new life into us; his comfort is enough for us.

Psalm 149

'Let them praise his name with dancing, making melody to him with tambourine and lyre. For the Lord takes pleasure in his people; he adorns the humble with victory.'

It is a gift to enjoy one another's company, to accept another in all their frailty and to rejoice. The very idea that the Lord might take pleasure in His people is an idea to set us dancing, and we see how humility is something very beautiful.

Outro

'If we want to read and pray the prayers of the Bible, and especially the Psalms, our first question must not be what have they to do with us, but what have they to do with Jesus Christ'. These words were written by the theologian Dietrich Bonhoeffer who was willing to give his life to help establish the Kingdom of God. For some today, Christ is not so central to faith; for others, He is the Beginning and the Ending of all things. We each find the way that brings us hope and comfort in dark times, and that will help us to share our moments of joy.

In the New Testament in the Bible, St. Paul wrote in his Letter to the Romans: "Who will separate us from the love of Christ? Will hardship, or distress, or persecution, or famine, or nakedness, or peril, or sword? [or Alzheimer's disease, or Parkinson's, or every dementia known to us?] No, in all these things we are more than conquerors through him who loved us, for I am convinced that neither death nor life, nor angels, nor rulers, nor things present, nor things to come, nor powers, not height, nor depth, nor anything else in all creation will be able to separate us from the love of God in Christ Jesus our Lord."

So here it is then, the best of all: we are completely safe in God's love.